T0198829

CROSSING COMPLETED

How the People of Eastham Saved Nauset Light

by Alice L. Shardlow

PHOTOGRAPHS BY
Alice L. Shardlow
and Shirley C. Sabin

Acknowledgements:

Many thanks to Shirley, Don, Avec, Michele, Dawn, Betty and Charlie, Hannah, Dee, Chris, and all others who listened and provided support.

To order additional copies of this book, contact:
Xlibris
844-714-8691
www.Xlibris.com
Orders@Xlibris.com

ISBN: Softcover   978-1-4257-1638-7

Library of Congress Control Number: 2006904257

Print information available on the last page

Rev. date: 09/05/2023

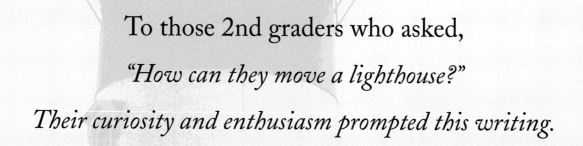

To those 2nd graders who asked,

"How can they move a lighthouse?"

Their curiosity and enthusiasm prompted this writing.

For my Grandchildren

Nauset Light's rotating beam blinked red,

blinked white, piercing the heaviness of fog.

On clear days, sailors at sea watched for the tower's daymark, painted red on top, white on the bottom. Built in 1877, the lighthouse was moved in 1923 to Nauset Bluff, an area named after the Native American Indian tribe living on Cape Cod more than three centuries ago. A few yards to the west, stood the red-roofed keeper's house covered with shingles grayed by salt air.

On the beach below, families spent summer days splashing in the surf, jumping breakers and shrieking with laughter. Salt water stung eyes, and sun parched skin.

Down the beach, away from the crowds, fishermen cast their lines, dreaming of a big catch.

Shore birds scampered along tide's edge, burrowing pointy beaks in search of a tidbit, their wings flapping and heads bobbing like whirligigs.

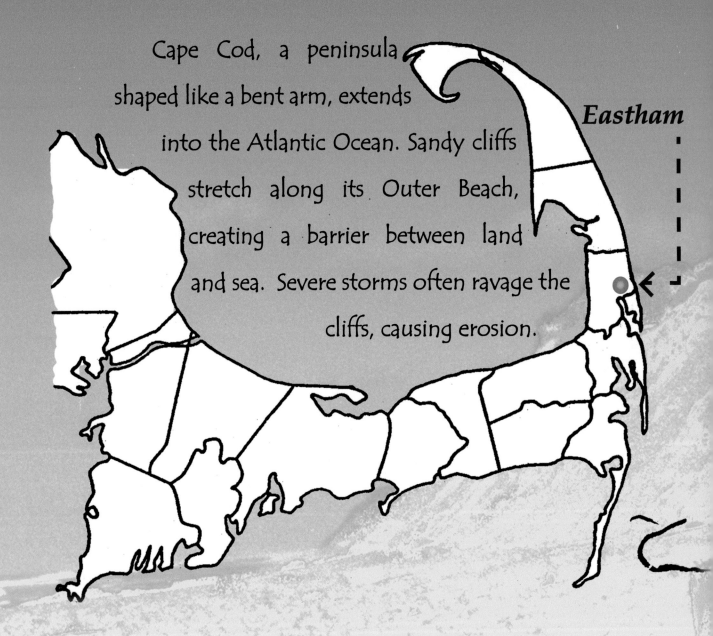

Cape Cod, a peninsula shaped like a bent arm, extends into the Atlantic Ocean. Sandy cliffs stretch along its Outer Beach, creating a barrier between land and sea. Severe storms often ravage the cliffs, causing erosion.

Eastham

For years, the dreaded Nor'easter riled the sea into salty foam, spewing water and tearing away great chunks of land, undermining the cliff where Nauset Light stood. Sand pelted the structure's cast iron walls and blew along the beach in dense, blinding sheets.

Over time, continued erosion narrowed the distance between the tower and cliff's edge until less than thirty-five feet of land remained. Unless rescued, the lighthouse was doomed to plummet into the ocean.

Many residents of Eastham, Massachusetts feared losing their lighthouse. They banded together as the Nauset Light Preservation Society raising money to move the tower across the road to safe ground. Society members worked tirelessly while the ocean continued eroding the cliff.

Three years later, on Saturday, October 12, 1996, sunlight reflected from shovel blades propped against Nauset Light. Officials stepped to the light's electrical panel and flicked the switch that controlled the rotating beam. Whir, whirrr, whwhhiirr, silence, darkness. A haunting stillness surrounded the cliff as shovels pierced the ground.

NAUSET LIGHT
MEMBER
PRESERVATION SOCIETY

The relocation work officially began the following Monday. The whine of a chain saw echoed through the woods on the other side of the road. Workers cut pine trees and cleared land.

Construction of a sandy roadway progressed, creating a firm surface for heavy machinery and trucks transporting construction materials to the site.

On the cliff, workers cut holes into Nauset Light's foundation with a tough, diamond tipped saw blade whistling through the old concrete. Steel beams were cut to fit with an acetylene torch.

When in place, they supported and stabilized the tower during the move.

Hydraulic jacks raised the tower seven feet in the air, allowing workers to stand beneath it. Huge wheeled dollies were slid underneath, preparing to roll the heavy load to the new site.

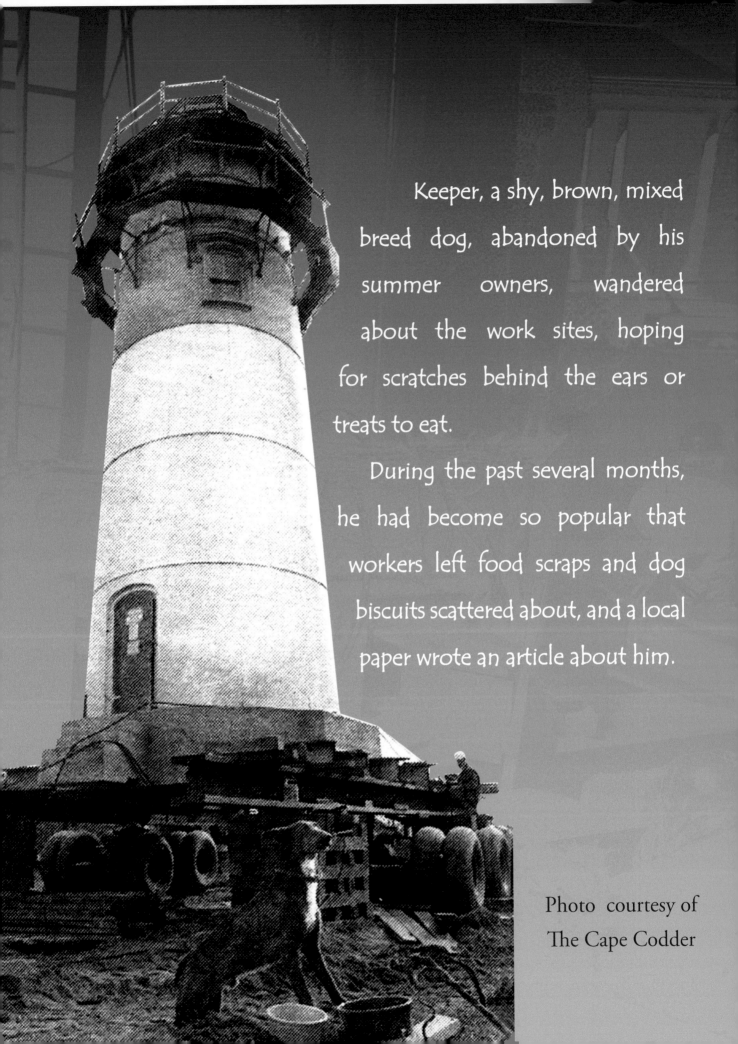

Keeper, a shy, brown, mixed breed dog, abandoned by his summer owners, wandered about the work sites, hoping for scratches behind the ears or treats to eat.

During the past several months, he had become so popular that workers left food scraps and dog biscuits scattered about, and a local paper wrote an article about him.

Late Friday morning, November 16, 1996, threatening clouds broke as spectators gathered on Nauset Light Beach Road. Bitter northwest wind crackled the brown oak leaves, and the golden beach grass swayed low, brushing sand like brooms. The long banner of thanks, hoisted high on the tower by Preservation Society members, flapped against the scaffolding surrounding the structure.

Throughout the after-noon, wind shivered up the backs of scurrying workmen. Observers, lined along work-zone barricades, dug in their pockets for gloves and mittens. Snowflakes blurred camera lenses and dotted workers' hard hats.

At 2:30 Valerie, the supervisor, bellowed, "OK!" Keeper, tail between legs, dashed to safety. Confused by all the commotion, he turned and ran back toward the lighthouse. Suddenly, in fear, he stopped! Crouching low, his belly skimmed the ground.

Overhead, a patch of blue briefly brightened the sky as the truck, backing through sandy soil, hooked onto the foundation dollies.

Gentle tug, nudge forward. Stronger tug, short moves. Soft sand sucked the truck's wheels. A sudden jerk and the tower leaned. Spectators gasped! To their relief, the stabilizers in the dollies did their job and kept the lighthouse upright.

Workers clustered to discuss the problem, knelt close to the jacked-up tower as if in prayer. They rose and laid thick wooden ties, like a railroad track, creating a solid surface in the sand for the chugging diesel truck. The driver inched his vehicle forward. Like a rocket ready for lift off, the lighthouse towered above the keeper's house. More starts and stops. Slowly Nauset Light rounded the corner of the house.

Evening clouds gathered on the horizon, hung over the sea, moved closer and hugged the shoreline. Spectators tightened scarves and huddled together for warmth, while the tower cautiously moved toward the road. Truck lights pierced through chilly evening air as the lighthouse crept at a snail's pace down the slope to rest for the night.

Mary, owner of the lighthouse keeper's home, was so concerned about Keeper's scrawny look, that she quietly placed a bowl of food on the porch steps. During the evening, he emptied it, crawled into the garage and curled up sleepily on the concrete floor.

Early Saturday morning, a smattering of onlookers gathered. Before the truck could haul the towering lighthouse onto the road, low-slung power lines needed to be disconnected. A power company worker, hoisted in a bucket to the top of the electric pole, dropped them safely to the roadside.

The truck driver jumped into the cab, revved the engine and inched onto the road with the 90-ton structure in tow.

A hush spread through the growing crowd as the lighthouse, crawling downhill, brushed the roadsides.

An hour and a half later, the driver turned right onto the sandy construction road.

Inching the tower along, Nauset Light finally came to rest over the new footing, an octagonal concrete ring in the ground.

Crossing completed!

Billowing clouds, streaked cotton-candy pink by the setting sun, hovered above. Weary workers turned off equipment, put tools away and left for the night. Relieved spectators and reporters walked to the parking lot.

In the stillness blanketing the cliff, Mary finally coaxed Keeper into the house. He crawled cautiously up the stairs and snuggled next to her golden lab. Safe and warm, he fell asleep.

>—‹•›—⊙—‹•›—‹

During the winter, as final stages of the process continued, Mary found a permanent home for Keeper. He loved spending long hours running across beach sand and barking at the waves.

At the new site, masons laid brick, closing holes where the temporary steel crossbeams had supported the moving lighthouse. Soil filled spaces around the tower's brick base until only the concrete foundation remained visible above ground. A concrete floor was poured inside and electricity reconnected.

Painters, lowered up and down on scaffolding, brightened the faded red and white exterior. Workers climbed the steep sides, like high wire acrobats, repairing the deck and installing an authentic glossy black iron railing.

A spring breeze ruffled the ocean Friday evening, May 10, 1997. Across the road, anticipation rippled through the crowd assembled to celebrate the relighting of Nauset Light. Before them the tower sparkled like a child going to a birthday party. Music filled the air and excitement swelled during the ceremony. At last, switches flicked.

Whwhhiirr, whirr, whir.
Blink red.   Blink white.
Joyful clapping and cheers
arose from the crowd, a
send-off to the flashing
beam once again skimming
Atlantic waves.

A Note from the Author:

It is hoped that this record will instill a desire to cherish and respect the historic structures of our land. Radar, satellites and computers have replaced lighthouses, but they remain an important part of our past, when keepers climbed steep stairs, lighting beams to safely guide those at sea. It is also a reminder that often people need to move on to find their own safe place. New beginnings are special gifts.

Today, Nauset Light is owned by the National Park Service and is operated as a private aid to navigation by the Nauset Light Preservation Society. It continues to be a special part of Cape Cod's history and the heritage of all Americans. Its beacon beckons visitors during the day and casts a protective beam over the cliff and ocean at night.

The keeper's house, now also owned by the National Park Service, was moved across the road three years later, once again joining its lighthouse companion.

During the summer, The Nauset Light Preservation Society conducts tours. A current schedule and new information is available by visiting the website:

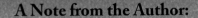

www.nausetlight.org

The Society may be contacted in writing at:

Nauset Light Preservation Society
P.O. Box 941
Eastham, MA 02642
Phone: (508) 240-2612
nausetlight@capecod.net

Additional information and newsletters about lighthouses are available through The United States Lighthouse Society which may be reached at:

244 Kearney Street, 5th Floor
San Francisco CA 94108

Printed in the United States
by Baker & Taylor Publisher Services